WI

JUL '92

The Porcupine

The Porcupine

By Victoria Sherrow

DILLON PRESS, INC.
Minneapolis, Minnesota 55415

Photographic Achnowledgments

The photographs are reproduced through the courtesy of: Peter V. August/American Society of Mammalogists; W. Perry Conway; Gerry Ellis/Ellis Wildlife Collection; Michael Francis/Ellis Wildlife Collection; Ron Garrison/San Diego Zoo; Minnesota Zoo; Jon R. Nichels/U.S. Fish and Wildlife Service; Leonard Lee Rue III; Len Rue, Jr.; Science Museum of Minnesota; Alan H. Shoemaker/Riverbanks Zoological Society of San Diego. Cover photo courtesy of Leonard Lee Rue III.

Library of Congress Cataloging-in-Publication Data

Sherrow, Victoria.
    The porcupine / by Victoria Sherrow.
      p. cm. — (A Dillon remarkable animals book)
    Includes bibliographical references.
    Summary: Examines the physical characteristics, habits, and
natural environment of the North American species of porcupine.
    ISBN 0-87518-442-1 (lib. bdg.)
    1. North American porcupine—Juvenile literature. 2. Porcupines—
Juvenile literature. [1. North American porcupine.
2. Porcupines.] I. Title. II. Series.
QL737.R652s28 1991
599.32'34—dc20   90-3278
                                           CIP
                                           AC

Dillon Press, Inc., 242 Portland Avenue South
Minneapolis, Minnesota 55415

Printed in the United States of America
1 2 3 4 5 6 7 8 9 10 99 98 97 96 95 94 93 92 91

Contents

Facts about the Porcupine

Scientific Names: *Hystricidae* (Old World porcupine)
Erethizontidae (New World porcupine)

Description:
Length—32 to 46 inches (80 to 115 centimeters) including the tail, which is 6 to 12 inches (15 to 30 centimeters) long
Height—About 12 inches (30 centimeters), measured from the foot to the shoulder
Weight—11 to 40 pounds (5 to 18.2 kilograms)
Physical Features—About 30,000 barbed quills on the tail and back; four long, sharp incisors for gnawing; sharp, curved claws and padded feet for climbing up and down trees
Color—Black, dark brown, or yellowish-white fur

Distinctive Habits: When attacked by an enemy, makes noises, lowers its head, and raises the quills on its back and tail; hits the enemy with its spiky tail; eats leaves and bark year-round; is active at night and during the winter

Food: Fruits, vegetables, leaves, bark, flowers, cactus, grasses, herbs; also eats water lilies and other plants that grow in water

Reproductive Cycle: Adults mate in the autumn; about seven months later, the female gives birth to one baby and raises it alone

Life Span: Nine to fifteen years

Range: Canada, the United States (Maine, New Hampshire, Vermont, Massachusetts, Connecticut, Maryland, West Virginia, Tennessee, Indiana, Michigan, Iowa, Texas, California, Oregon, Washington, and Alaska), Mexico, Central America, South America, Asia, Africa, Indonesia

The shaded areas on the map show the range of the porcupine.

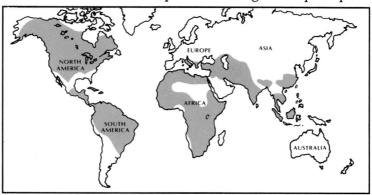

North American porcupines appear soft, fluffy, and harmless but are, in fact, some of the best-protected animals on earth.

Chapter 1

Nature's Walking Pincushion

Scratch, scratch. Rustle, rustle. A black-haired animal with orange teeth makes soft noises as it steps out of a hollow tree trunk. As moonlight fills the October sky, the porcupine leaves its home in the oak tree to look for food.

A stray dog in the woods sees the porcupine shuffle along. The dog moves closer and sniffs. The porcupine's eyes are set wide apart. It cannot see objects more than several feet ahead, so it does not know what animal is sniffing about. But its keen nose smells trouble.

Sensing danger, the porcupine turns its back toward the dog. It tucks its head between its front legs, chatters its teeth, and arches its back. Thousands of **quills*** stand up, like needles, on the

---

* Words in **bold type** are explained in the glossary at
  the end of this book.

porcupine's back and tail. The quills rattle against one another, as the porcupine shakes its body. Then the porcupine smacks the dog with its tail.

The dog whines and bites at the quills. But the painful quills have stuck in its skin and will not come out. The unhappy dog runs away, leaving the porcupine alone and in peace once again.

Self Protection

(The porcupine is one of the best-protected animals on earth. It has about 30,000 quills—hard, stiff hairs with sharp, pointed ends. Quills cover the animal's whole body, except for the face and the stomach.)

When the porcupine is not in danger, the quills lie flat beneath an outer coat of **guard hairs**. Guard hairs are softer than quills and help support them when they are raised. In winter, guard hairs grow longer to keep the porcupine warm.

Quills that grow around an adult porcupine's face are about .5 inch (1.3 centimeters) long, and

The quills on a porcupine's face are shorter than those on the rest of its body.

those on the tail are about 3 inches (7.5 centimeters) long. Quills grow to their full length in about three months. They are loose in the porcupine's skin and come out easily when it shakes its tail at an enemy.

Some kinds of porcupines have **barbs** on the

tips of their quills. Much like fish hooks, barbs make quills hard to pull out of skin. When the quills are pulled, the sharp barbs spread out and hold tight underneath the skin. That is why it hurts to remove porcupine quills.

People who get stuck with quills can remove them with pliers. An animal doctor can do the same for a family pet. But wild animals are not so lucky. The quills in their bodies soak up liquids and swell. At times, they travel to important organs, such as the lungs or the brain. When this happens, the animal will likely die. It can also starve if quills are stuck in its mouth, which makes eating much too painful.

Long, Sharp Teeth

Inside the porcupine's mouth is a set of amazing teeth. In each jaw are two long teeth called **incisors**, that are designed for cutting and gnawing. Incisors keep growing throughout the porcupine's life. The animal keeps these teeth from growing too long by grinding them against each other as it chews its food. Gnawing on hard foods, such as bark, keeps the incisors sharp.

Porcupines are **herbivores**, or plant-eating animals. Finding food is not a problem during warm months, when tree shoots, leaves, grasses, fruits, and vegetables are growing. But during the winter, bark may be the only plant food around. A porcupine's long, sharp incisors are able to chew bark, helping the animal to eat during every season.

The porcupine also has **molars**—flat teeth designed for grinding—in the back of its mouth to chew tough food. It has strong, heavy jaw muscles, too. Incisors, molars, and strong jaws allow the porcupine to eat bark in the winter, when some other animals starve because few plants grow at this time of year.

Climbing Up, Up, Up!

The porcupine looks slow and clumsy on the

Porcupines are skilled climbers.

ground, but it is a good climber. This spiky animal
can climb 50 to 60 feet (15.3 to 18.3 meters) high in
a tree! Its front feet have four toes each, and the
hind feet have five. Each toe has a sharp, curved
claw that grips bark and grasps branches.

A porcupine's feet and legs are good for climbing in many ways. Each foot has a rough pad on the bottom to keep the porcupine from slipping. The porcupine wraps its legs around a tree trunk. Then it pulls itself up, with one leg first, and then the other. Its legs may be short, but they are strong!

The porcupine's tail is strong, too. It has a clump of stiff bristles underneath, like a scrub brush or a back brush. By pressing these bristles against a tree, the porcupine balances itself.

The porcupine is careful as it climbs out on a branch to munch bark or leaves. It tests the branch before moving out further, in case the branch is too weak to hold its weight. People who watch porcupines say that these animals seem to remember which limbs on trees are safe to climb.

Now and then, a porcupine falls from a tree. It may forget to test a branch. Young porcupines may fall before they learn safe ways to climb up and down. They sometimes break a rib or a leg bone, but these broken bones usually heal.

The porcupine's air-filled quills help make the animal a good swimmer.

Time for a Swim

The porcupine's quills are more than a weapon—they help the animal swim, too. In warm weather, a porcupine may see yellow water lilies or other tasty-looking plants in a stream or pond. The porcupine waddles into the water and swims toward the plant food. The tubelike quills have a spongy material inside them. The airy filling helps the porcupine to float on the surface of the water.

Swimming helps protect the porcupine. When an enemy threatens, the porcupine sometimes heads for the water. It swims away, leaving its enemy standing alone on the bank.

Whether shuffling into a lake or strolling along in the woods, a porcupine looks tame. It appears to be soft and even "petable." But beneath its hairy coat are thousands of sharp quills, ready to rise at the threat of danger. The animal that bothers a porcupine will be sorry!

The porcupine family has lived on earth for 35 million years.

Chapter 2

A Closer Look at the "Quill Pig"

It may seem strange that a family of animals that moves slowly and sees poorly has managed to survive for millions of years. But with help from its sharp teeth and barbed quills, the porcupine has been able to do just that.

Scientists think that porcupines have lived in South America and in Europe for about 35 million years. About 2 to 4 million years ago, some traveled north from South America. They made their homes in the many wooded areas of the regions where the United States and Canada are today.

Through the years, people have had some false ideas about porcupines. A common belief is that porcupines can shoot their quills at enemies. A famous American poet, Henry Wadsworth

Longfellow, wrote a poem in the 1800s called "The Song of Hiawatha." In the poem, he described an animal that "shot its shining quills, like arrows." No doubt Longfellow meant the porcupine in this part of his poem.

But, in fact, porcupine quills do not shoot out of a porcupine's skin. They only appear as if they do—when the animal shakes its tail and loose quills fall out of its tail skin.

A Special Rodent

The porcupine's common name comes from its most famous body part—its quills. The word "porcupine" comes from the French words *porc*, which means pig, and *epine*, meaning spine. Spine is another word for thorn or quill. That is why porcupines are sometimes called "quill pigs."

What do porcupines have in common with pigs? Maybe people once thought that the porcupine's big nostrils and snorting noises were like those of a pig. But unlike pigs, porcupines are

rodents. The **order**, or group, of animals called *rodentia* includes rats, rabbits, hamsters, squirrels, and beavers. The porcupine is the second biggest rodent living in North America. The largest is the beaver.

Rodents are best known for their teeth. All rodents have four long, orange or yellow-colored incisors.

Different Kinds of Porcupines

Scientists divide porcupines into two main groups. New World porcupines live in North and South America. Old World porcupines live across the Atlantic Ocean—in Africa, Asia, and Europe. There are 7 **species**, or kinds, of New World porcupines and 21 Old World species.

The North American porcupine is a New World porcupine. This species has the scientific name *Erethizon dorsatum*, which means "the one whose back rises in anger" in Latin.

Adult North American porcupines are about

30 to 40 inches (75 to 100 centimeters) long, including their tails, which are 6 to 8 inches (15 to 20 centimeters) in length. They stand about 1 foot (31 centimeters) high when measured from foot to shoulder, and weigh between 11 to 20 pounds (5 to 9.1 kilograms). Porcupines that live in the western United States often weigh more—as much as 30 to 40 pounds (13.6 to 18.2 kilograms).

North American porcupines live mainly in pine forests in the northern United States and across Canada (south of the Yukon Territory). These forests lie both in valleys and in mountainous areas. North American porcupines are **nocturnal** animals, meaning they are active at night. They are known, too, for their **arboreal** life-style—they climb and live in trees.

Another species of New World porcupine climbs trees even better than its relatives in North America. Tree porcupines live in the tropical **rain forests** of Central and South America. Like the North American porcupine, the Tree porcupine is

Tree porcupines have useful, long tails.

a nocturnal, plant-eating animal. During the day, it hides in hollow logs or in **burrows**—holes dug in the ground. These burrows are dug by other animals, not by the porcupine. Most porcupines are not good diggers.

The Tree porcupine's tail is not very helpful in protecting the animal. The bottom half of its tail has no quills. But it is useful for climbing trees. It is a **prehensile** tail, meaning it is able to grasp tree branches. A Tree porcupine can hang from a branch and swing by its tail, like a monkey.

If an enemy comes near a Tree porcupine, the porcupine stands up on its hind legs. It snarls angrily. If the enemy attacks, the porcupine will bite it or try to slap it with the quills on its back.

The Fiercest Porcupine

The best-known Old World porcupine is the Crested porcupine. It lives in Asia and North Africa. This spiky creature is more dangerous than its North American relatives.

Some of the Crested porcupine's quills grow 12 to 15 inches (31 to 38.5 centimeters) long! They are hollow, very sharp, and may be as thick as soda straws. The black and silvery-striped quills sparkle when they move.

African Crested porcupines have a crest of hair growing on top of their heads. That is how this species got its name.

Crested porcupines measure about 3 feet (.9 meter) from head to tail. A large male can weigh as much as 50 pounds (22.7 kilograms). These animals do not climb trees as North American porcupines do. They live among the cracks of rocks, or in burrows that they dig in the ground. Two or more Crested porcupines often share the same underground home. Unlike most species, Crested porcupines are good diggers. Their burrows can be as long as 30 to 50 feet (9.2 to 15.3 meters).

Other animals must take care when they are near this species of porcupine. Unlike the North American species, a Crested porcupine does not just stand still when an enemy appears. It warns an enemy by raising its quills, and rattling them against each other. If the enemy does not run away, the Crested porcupine charges! It turns

A North African Crested porcupine.

around, runs backward, and stabs its attacker with its quills. These long, very sharp quills are deadly. Even strong lions have died from them.

Another Old World porcupine, the Brush-tailed porcupine of Asia and Africa, was named for the hairs at the end of its tail. Its thin, flat quills

form a bundle, like a brush. Brush-tailed porcupines live in forests, but they are not arboreal.
They make their homes among roots at the bases
of large trees. These porcupines are about 2.5 feet
(.8 meter) long from head to tail, and they weigh
about 5 pounds (2.3 kilograms).

Porcupines Are Not Hedgehogs!

Sometimes people confuse the porcupine with
the hedgehog. Hedgehogs are small animals, about
9 inches (22.5 centimeters) long. They have
brownish-black hair and spines, or quills, on their
backs.

Hedgehogs live in Europe and are quite different from porcupines. They are not active in the
winter as porcupines are. They eat animals, such
as mice, instead of plants. And a hedgehog protects
itself by rolling into a tight, prickly ball on the
ground.

An experienced animal-watcher can tell a
hedgehog from a porcupine. But it takes years of

A hedgehog.

careful study to learn much more about the quiet, nocturnal porcupine. By studying this amazing family of animals, scientists have learned how it has managed to survive in the world's forests for 35 million years.

Chapter 3

A Quiet Life in the Forest

A cold wind blows as a North American porcupine walks slowly across the snow. It climbs a pine tree to chew a winter meal of bark. As the porcupine eats, small pieces of branches fall to the ground. These wood chips will not go to waste. The rabbits in the forest are hungry, too.

Winter is a harsh season in this New England forest. But throughout the year, porcupines manage to find food and shelter here.

Porcupines are active all winter long. They are not good diggers, so they must find ready-made shelters—old tree stumps, hollow trees, or deep cracks among rocks. They might also live in caves, other animals' empty dens, or deserted houses.

During the winter, more than one porcupine

North American porcupines eat bark to survive during winter months when food is scarce.

may share a den. But they prefer to live alone. If a porcupine moves into a relative's den, the relative may leave to find another private place.

Small, Protected Areas

Porcupines do not travel far from their chosen homes. A porcupine can walk only about 2 miles (3.2 kilometers) in an hour. Its short legs that are curved outward cause its waddling walk.

Many porcupines stay in a small area year-round. One might even stay in the same tree through the fall and the winter, if it finds enough food there. It will defend its favorite feeding tree from other animals that try to eat its bark.

Sometimes a porcupine walks a few miles to escape a bad snowstorm, to find food, or find a mate. A porcupine that lives in the mountains during warm months may move to lower valleys in the winter. Here, there are more trees to eat, and the weather is less harsh. But porcupines usually stay within an area of about 20 to 30 acres (8 to 12 hectares). In the wintertime, they often stay in a smaller area, about 6 acres (2.4 hectares) large.

A porcupine protects itself in this **territory** in several ways, besides using its quills. It gets some protection from its brown or black fur, which blends with the dark color of tree trunks. This blending acts as **camouflage**, helping to hide the animal. Enemies pass by without noticing it.

Porcupines also avoid many enemies because the spiky rodents are active at night. Eating in a tree after dark, the porcupine is hidden among the tangled, leafy branches. The only signs that it is there are munching sounds, or bits of branches that fall to the ground as it eats.

Problems With Predators

What animal would be foolish enough to fight with a porcupine? Many wild animals know they should leave porcupines alone. But some hungry animals attack and kill the porcupine. They are its **predators,** or animals that hunt it for food.

The porcupine must defend itself against many predators, such as bears, foxes, bobcats, wolverines, coyotes, mountain lions, weasels, eagles, and horned owls. These animals are sometimes found dead with quills in their bodies, showing that they lost fights with the prickly rodents.

Porcupines living in Africa must watch out for lions and tigers. But the fierce Crested porcupine often wins battles with these larger animals.

The animal that most often succeeds in killing a porcupine is the fisher, a large member of the weasel family. Fishers are furry animals with bushy tails. They weigh about 5 to 10 pounds (2.3 to 4.5 kilograms) and are smaller than most porcupines.

People once thought that a fisher killed a porcupine by pushing it onto its back, and attacking its unhairy stomach. But people have learned that fishers attack the larger rodent's head instead. The quick-footed fisher races back and forth, nip-

Through the years, the North American porcupine's main enemy has been the quick-footed fisher.

ping at the porcupine's face. After defending itself for a while, the porcupine cannot fight any longer. The fisher wins the battle and gains a porcupine meal.

Other Dangers

Porcupines face risks from diseases and harsh weather, as well as from predators. Some porcupines die in the wintertime from starvation. A porcupine may find enough bark to fill its stomach during cold months. But this narrow diet lacks important **nutrients**—vitamins, minerals, or proteins that are necessary for healthy growth. The porcupine can become weak during harsh weather, and begin to move slowly. It might freeze to death or be attacked by another hungry animal, because it is too weak to raise its quills and defend itself.

Porcupines can get sick or have accidents, too. They are sometimes hit by cars when crossing roads. And some get an illness called **snuffles**—

a flu-like disease that affects animals—that can lead to death from **pneumonia**, a lung disease.

Porcupines also suffer from **parasites**, tiny animals such as lice and ticks, that live on their skin and feed on their blood. Worms sometimes live in their stomachs, too, eating their food. Parasites cause porcupines to feel sick, but do not kill them.

Through the years, porcupines have lived on in spite of these problems. Today, they are not in danger of becoming extinct, or dying out. In spite of their large numbers, though, they are hard to spot in their forest homes. A person might walk in the same woods every day, and still not see any porcupines. The spiky rodents are likely sleeping, or quietly minding their own business.

Chapter 4

Porcupines Through the Year

A female porcupine stretches on a limb of a red oak tree. It is a cool October night, and there are delicious acorns to pick and eat. Throughout the month, she gains weight from acorns and other nuts. Nuts have taken the place of the juicy apples she ate in September.

Every night, the porcupine climbs out to reach the nut-covered branches. In the daytime, she sleeps on an oak branch or in a hollow tree trunk on the ground.

The New England air is now misty and quite cold. In November, a male approaches her and makes whining noises. He begins to chase her, but she raises her quills in warning.

Another male approaches. The female por-

In the fall, the porcupine eats many apples, acorns, and nuts to gain extra weight that will help it survive the lean winter months.

cupine whines, moans, and chatters her teeth. The male whines, too. The two porcupines rub their noses together. They touch each other with their front paws. They have chosen each other as mates.

This male and female stay together for the next few days. They do a special mating dance, rocking back and forth on their hind feet.

After mating, the male porcupine leaves. The female will live alone as before, until her baby is born in the spring.

Brrr—Winter!

The air grows frosty as winter arrives in the forest. Even when the temperature drops below freezing, the female porcupine stays active. But it is harder now for her to find food. Her feet and tail leave prints on the fluffy, white snow as she visits her favorite hemlock tree to eat. If deep snow covers the ground, she will stay in this tree until the weather improves. She will sleep on a branch during the day.

The female porcupine usually eats from just one or two favorite trees near her den. When she returns to her den, she may step in the same tracks to save energy. She has already lost some of the fat that she gained during the warmer months. Porcupines lose about one-third of their normal weight in the wintertime.

The porcupine depends upon her fur coat to protect her from the cold. This fur grows thicker during the winter. In the springtime, the porcupine begins to **molt,** or shed, the winter fur. Within three or four months, the old fur will be gone. A new, lighter coat will take its place.

Spring Warms the Forest

When the snow melts in the springtime, the porcupine smells growing plants. After her winter diet of bark, she desires soft, green buds and leaves on oaks, sugar maples, and other forest trees. She will also enjoy mouth-watering herbs and grasses that now grow from the ground.

The porcupine's fur grows thicker and longer in the wintertime to protect the animal from the cold.

An owl hoots as the porcupine feasts on these spring treats. This green diet has vitamins and other nutrients that she needs. The nutrients are good for both her and the baby porcupine that will be born in about a month.

In May, the female porcupine gives birth to

one baby. This will be the female's only baby this year. It is called a **porcupette**. The baby comes into the world with its eyes already open. It weighs about one pound (.5 kilogram) and is nearly one foot long. It can walk by itself in less than an hour.

The porcupette has eight teeth and its own set of quills. The quills are not hard when the porcupette is born. But just 30 to 40 minutes after the birth, the quills become stiff enough so that the baby could defend itself from an attack.

The female porcupine and her baby nest in an open space between rocks. Here, the porcupette drinks its first meal of warm milk from its mother. It continues to drink this milk for about 3 to 4 weeks. But after two weeks, it is able to munch tender leaves and grass, too.

At night, the two-week-old porcupette follows its mother to look for food. They nibble leaves, twigs, herbs, and wild berries.

The porcupette is curious and playful. It peeks under logs and bushes to see what might be there.

A female Malayan porcupine and her porcupette.

It squeals and grunts as it finds another porcupette in the woods. The porcupettes chase each other in circles. Later, the porcupette enjoys its first swim, paddling into a pond to eat water lily stems.

A Porcupette Grows Up

The porcupette soon learns to be an excellent tree-climber. At first, it will not follow its mother up a tree. She has to keep calling her baby. But now, the porcupette grips the bark with its claws and climbs up. It climbs back down tail first, using the stiff brush under its tail for support.

The porcupette has also learned how to find different kinds of food. Garden crops, such as lettuce, carrots, and beans, are tasty finds. The greater supply of food in the summer helps the porcupette to gain weight. When it is four weeks old, it weighs about two pounds (.9 kilogram).

The porcupette learns, too, to watch out for danger. One night, a fox appears in the woods. The female porcupine turns her back to the fox,

puts her head between her paws, and raises her quills. The porcupette does the same thing. When the fox reaches out, the mother slaps him with her prickly tail. The fox backs away, whining. The porcupines are safe.

The two-month-old porcupette is now ready to leave its mother. It is old enough to make its own way in the forest. As autumn approaches, the young porcupine looks for a den and for its own food supply.

With its remarkable quills, clawed feet, and sharp teeth, this young porcupine is well-suited for life in the woods. It will mate after it is three years old. Once again, a baby quill pig will be born and will learn to live quietly among the trees.

Young porcupines learn how to find different kinds of food, such as springtime buds on tree branches.

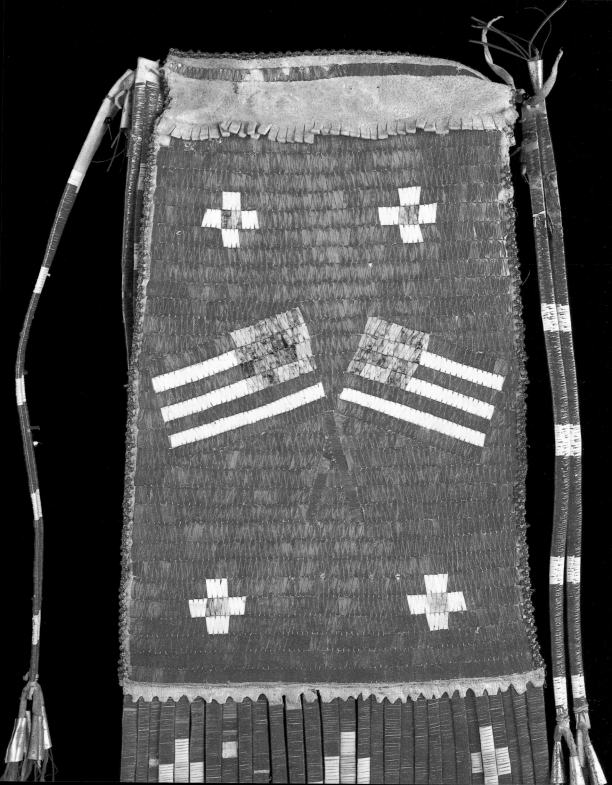

Chapter 5

Porcupines and People

Hundreds of years ago, people ate porcupines. Native Americans caught the prickly animals and carried them home in sacks. They ate the flesh and used the quills to decorate baskets, moccasins, and headdresses. Some tribes dyed the quills with the juices of berries and other plants. Early American settlers and hunters used the porcupine for food, too.

In more recent years, people have viewed the porcupine as less of a blessing. In fact, many people have called it a pest. People rarely spot porcupines, but they are sometimes bothered by things that these animals do.

Those long teeth that are so handy for year-round eating can get the porcupine in trouble

A pipe bag made by Eastern Dakota Native Americans in the early 1900s. They wrapped dyed porcupine quills around strips of deerskin to make the bag.

49

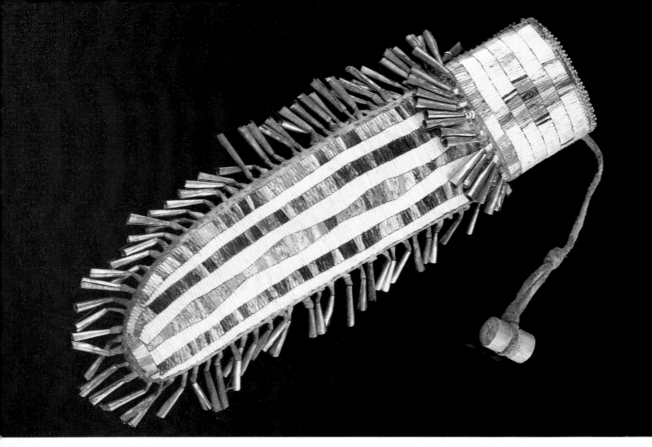

A knife case made by Eastern Dakota Native Americans in the mid-1800s, using porcupine quills, deerskin, and buffalo rawhide.

with people. Porcupines eat farm crops, such as corn, carrots, and potatoes. They climb trees in orchards, and eat apples and other fruits. They eat garden flowers, too, such as geraniums.

People also get upset when porcupines ruin trees by eating the bark. During the winter, a porcupine may chew all around a tree trunk, through the layers of bark that hold sap. Sap contains sugar and starch that feed the tree. It travels down from the leaves where it is made and through the bark. If a porcupine chews all around the trunk, the tree will die above the circle of chewed-off bark.

Porcupines annoy some campers and home-owners, too. These spiky creatures love things that taste salty. They visit campgrounds, boat docks, cabins, and barns, where they chew up shoes, gloves, paddles, ax handles, and even wooden steps—anything that tastes salty from the touch of human skin.

People who think of porcupines as pests some-times decide to kill them. They set out traps or poison, or shoot them with guns. During the twentieth century, some state governments paid people to kill this animal. In the 1950s and 1960s, the governments of Vermont and Montana brought extra fishers into their forests. They knew

Porcupines seem to prefer things that taste salty, including this old soup can left behind by campers at a campground.

that these animals were the porcupine's worst enemies.

Prickly Pets
Other people like the porcupine. Some have raised baby porcupines as pets. If a female porcupine is

killed, its very young porcupette cannot live on its own. Sometimes a person finds and adopts it.

Taking care of these prickly pets can be tricky. A newborn must be fed with milk from a medicine dropper. The porcupette raises its quills when it is afraid, so people must wear thick gloves when holding it.

People with pet porcupines say they are playful and friendly. They can learn to come when someone calls their name. When they feel safe, they do not raise their quills around family members.

It is easy to find food for pet porcupines. They eat scraps of fruits, vegetables, nuts, and salad greens. One man who raised an orphaned porcupine said that his pet loved cookies and potato chips!

Pet porcupines do a lot of chewing, though. Owners of porcupines must be careful to hide their shoes and boots. They must keep their pets out of the vegetable and flower gardens, too.

Some people raise baby porcupines as pets.

These people have learned another important thing: movement from behind startles a porcupine, and it will raise its quills in alarm. These people know that they should always pet a porcupine from front to back!

Porcupines in the Future

Although a baby porcupine can become a family pet, most people agree that these animals belong in their forest homes. In nature, a porcupine lives a quiet life. It does not bother other creatures unless they attack first.

During a female porcupine's lifetime of 9 to 15 years, she has only about 6 to 12 babies. Unlike many other animals, porcupines do not have a large number of babies. But the small number of porcupettes usually remain alive and unharmed. They are strong, and can easily protect themselves with their quills.

This remarkable animal family has survived for 35 million years. Scientists who study animals believe it will continue to do so for many years to come. After all, a porcupine carries built-in protection, day and night. For millions of years, these stiff, sharp quills have meant the same thing: do not touch!

Glossary

arboreal (ahr-BORE-eeh-uhl)—living in trees

barb—a sharp point that is attached to an object and sticks out backwards; arrows, fish hooks, and some porcupine quills have barbs

burrow—a tunnel or hole dug in the ground by an animal, where it or other animals live and hide

camouflage (CAM-uh-flahj)—an appearance, especially color, that blends with the surroundings and may serve to conceal, or hide, an animal

guard hairs—hairs on a porcupine that are softer than quills and help to keep the animal warm

herbivore (UHR-buh-vore)—an animal that eats plants

incisor (in-SIE-zuhr)—a front tooth that is large and sharp, used for cutting or gnawing

molar—a large tooth that is flat on top, designed for grinding food; molars grow in the back of a person or animal's mouth

molt—to shed fur or skin which is replaced with a new coat or skin

nocturnal (nock-TURN-uhl)—active during the night

nutrient (NOO-tree-ehnt)—a vitamin, mineral, protein, or other substance found in food that helps support a living person, animal, or plant

order—a group of related people, animals, or things; lizards and snakes belong to the same order

parasite (PAIR-uh-site)—tiny creatures, such as mites, that live on larger animals; mites and other parasites feed on the larger animal, sucking its blood

pneumonia (noo-MOHN-yuh)—a serious disease of the lungs

porcupette (pork-yoo-PET)—a baby porcupine

predator (PREHD-uh-tuhr)—an animal that hunts other animals for food

prehensile (pree-HEN-suhl)—able to seize or grasp by wrapping around; a prehensile tail wraps around tree branches or leaves and helps the animal keep its balance

quill—a stiff, sharp hair on a porcupine or other such animal; the porcupine uses its quills to protect itself against attack

rain forest—a dense, humid tropical forest; occurs in areas that have high rainfall throughout the year

rodent (ROH-duhnt)—one of a large family of animals with four sharp front teeth used for cutting and gnawing

snuffles—a flu-like disease that affects animals; snuffles may develop into pneumonia

species (SPEE-sheez)—distinct kinds of individual plants or animals that have common characteristics and share a common name

territory—an area of land; wild animals defend their territory from other animals of the same kind

Index

About the Author

A lifelong student of nature, Victoria Sherrow received her Bachelor of Science and Master of Science degrees from Ohio State University. Today, she is a member of several environmental groups, including the Audubon Society and the National Wildlife Federation. Ms. Sherrow is also a member of the Society of Children's Book Writers. She has written many articles and short stories for children's magazines. *The Porcupine* is her fourth book for children. The author also wrote *The Gecko*, another Remarkable Animals book. Ms. Sherrow lives in Westport, Connecticut, with her husband and three children.